From
INMATE
to
PURPOSE

AKILA GILYARD

FROM INMATE TO PURPOSE

AKILA GILYARD

Copyright © 2021 by Akila Gilyard

All rights reserved.

Published by Firebrand Publishing Atlanta, GA USA

No part of this book may be reproduced in any form or by any electronic or mechanical means, including information storage and retrieval systems, without written permission from the author, except for the use of brief quotations in a book review and certain other noncommercial uses permitted by copyright law. For permission requests, write to the publisher, addressed "Attention: Permissions coordinator," at the email address: support@firebrandpublishing.com

Limit of Liability/Disclaimer of Warranty: While the publisher and author have used their best efforts in preparing this book, they make no representations or warranties with respect to the accuracy or completeness of the contents of this book and specifically disclaim any implied warranties of merchantability or fitness for a particular purpose. No warranty may be created or extended by sales representatives or written sales materials. The advice and strategies contained herein may not be suitable for your situation. You should consult with a professional where appropriate. Neither the publisher nor the author shall be liable for damages arising here from.

Firebrand Publishing publishes in a variety of print and electronic formats and by print-on-demand. For more information about Firebrand Publishing products, visit https://firebrandpublishing.com

ISBN: 978-1-941907-34-4 paperback

ISBN: 978-1-941907-32-0 ebook

Cover designed by Miblart

Printed in the United States of America

From Inmate to Purpose is dedicated to everyone that feels lost and feel like there is no way out.

I wrote this book in hopes to inspire ,intrigue, give hope, motivate, to never give up, to never give in, to take back the narrative of your life so that you may reach the results that you want and desire. You can do it.

I want to shout out my team and to everyone that ever told me, "No".

I appreciate you.

Contents

Preface	xi
Chapter 1	1
Chapter 2	7
Chapter 3	11
Chapter 4	19
Chapter 5	31
Chapter 6	41
Chapter 7	45
Chapter 8	59
Chapter 9	65
Chapter 10	75
About the Author	83
Notes	85

Preface

Well, I'm finally here. I'm finally at a place in my life where I can share what I've gone through. What I've done. What has helped me. What I wish I would have done better. I know a lot of people are going to pick up this book to be nosey. That's cool, I am kind of spilling the tea on my entire experience within the prison system. Some people are curious. That's also cool, because I appreciate the coin.

But for just a second, I want to make sure that I acknowledge the person who picked up this book hoping that it might inspire. This book is

Preface

written for the one who has been through something and doesn't quite know how to recover. This book is for the single mother struggling to make ends meet, be a good mother, and provide for her family all at the same time. Soon, you will come to realize that I have been through *a lot*. And I'm not just saying that to sound good.

Not only have I been through a lot, but I've gotten *myself* into compromising situations that I didn't have the power to get out of.

Sound like you? I was hoping so. Listen, throughout this book, I want to share with you some of my deepest, darkest moments. I want to share with you the anger, bitterness, nervousness, and every emotion and thought in between that I struggled with during the most pivotal moments in my life.

It's not all negative. I intend to share the beauty of it all, the grace I've experienced, and the lessons I've learned. Because of these experiences, I've been able to do things with my life and for my children that I never believed I could, and I hope that inspire you not to give up, no matter how bad it feels like things have gotten.

So, grab your popcorn, your soda, your tea, your rolls, whatever you need to get through this book because I'm going to take you back to where it all ended, and thus where it all began.

Chapter One

When I got my bearings, all I could see was the blood. He was clutching his throat, gasping for breath, eyes wide open.

I had blacked out. I didn't plan to cut him, that's just how things went down. He came at me. I defended myself. That's it.

I was sixteen-years-old, living what I thought was my best life if you had asked me at the time. I had moved in with my twenty-six-year-old boyfriend and our thirteen-month-old son. I was a high school dropout. On the outside looking in, it wasn't ideal, but it was where I had ended up and I was trying to make the best of it all.

On the afternoon of January 11, 2003, I came home not realizing that what would happen next would change my life forever. It was like any other day. I came home, expecting to be greeted by my significant other, the man who was sharing a bed with me. What I found instead, was him sharing our bed with someone else. I remember walking in on what was about to go down with him and this woman like it was a scene straight from a Lifetime movie.

I kept my composure for a while. He was a slick talker, so he tried to manipulate the situation to assure me that "nothing was going to happen." I may have been young, but I wasn't stupid.

Our argument made its way outside as he and this woman hopped into his car to leave. Something in me snapped when I watched him get into that car with her and drive away. Something inside me realized the foolishness that I had just experienced and all the bullshit that this man was trying to get me to believe.

I got in my car and followed them. At his point, I don't know if I was completely aware of what I was doing. I wasn't really sure what I was going to do as I followed them. But I drove. I followed them, thoughts racing through my mind, none of them making any sense. My rage had taken over. I saw red. I waited until we were on a road with minimal traffic and ran his car off the road. I know, it was definitely a crazy, Lifetime lady move. But I did it. With my baby in the backseat, I ran his father off the road.

Don't worry, it gets better, because I didn't stop there. For some reason, that wasn't enough to satisfy the rage burning inside of me in that moment. For some reason, after running him off the road, I proceeded to get out of my car. I don't remember picking up the box cutter. I don't remember where my mindset was. I vaguely remember him charging towards me. Slice. I cut his throat from the back of his ear to about two inches from his jugular. I guess I cut him pretty deep.

When I got my bearings, all I could see was the blood. He was clutching his throat, gasping for breath, eyes wide open. I had blacked out. I hadn't planned to cut him, that's just how things went down. He came at me. I defended myself.

People always ask me if I did anything to the girl, but the response is simple: No. I didn't do anything to her. She was never my problem. He was. I wasn't in a relationship with her. For all I knew, he had lied to her too. It's not like I knew who she was personally. No, I couldn't have cared less about her. He was the one I trusted. He was the one I shared a child with.

I want to take a moment to address the women reading this who may have been lied to or cheated on and blamed the women. We have to stop blaming the other woman for the dirt our dudes do. It's not her fault, most of the time. Most of the time, she doesn't know about you just like you didn't know about her.

After that, I remember getting back into my car, drenched in his blood, and driving my son to my mom's house. At that point, my thoughts were racing, this time out of worry instead of rage. I knew I wouldn't have very long to get a few affairs in order, and I knew I had just gravely messed up.

"I need you to watch my baby." That was all I could say to my mom when I barged into the house.

"What's going on? What happened?" She was screaming, trying to figure out what was happening. She was visibly upset and rightfully so. I had just walked into her house covered in blood to drop off my son with little explanation. I did try to prepare her a little bit knowing that the other woman would be calling the police.

Once I knew my son was in good hands, I calmly drove back to the home I shared with his father and waited. I really wasn't *that* calm. Pure nervousness was a more accurate description. I *knew* that whatever happened next wasn't going to be good.

Chapter Two

I was fifteen-years-old when my life changed drastically. I had my son. At this point, in the eyes of the church I had grown up in, I was a sinner. The path I had taken was the complete opposite of what the church had probably intended for me, but there was no changing it once my son was brought into the world.

Growing up, I was known in school as the girl who wasn't allowed to wear pants. For whatever reason, the church I was forced to go to believed that women who wore pants were sinners. They were considered loose, which in my mind never really made sense. The way I understood it, I was privier to giving it up in a skirt with easy access than I was in pants, right? Because of the strict limitations placed on us girls, I wasn't really allowed to go many places or do many things.

I didn't have a lot of friends growing up, and I think this led to a lot of resentment for not only God but for my mother as well. I hated the church, I hated the way I was being forced to live because I just knew that it wasn't right. At least not for me.

Maybe that was why I felt such rage seeing him with that women. Maybe that explains the anger that I felt that day. I had a lot of resentment built up inside of me. I was fifteen, a mother, a high school dropout, and now I was being faced with the actions of a man I had placed all my trust into. I was young and scared of having to do it all on my own. I didn't want to keep living according to how other people saw fit, and the continued betrayal of everyone in my life was starting to take its toll on me. I had been lied to for most of my life, I had been taken advantage of, and I think this whole situation was just the straw that broke the camel's back.

My relationships with my mother wasn't normal, and I felt like we were never really able to connect in the ways that a mother and daughter should. It always felt like nothing I did was enough. I was never enough. She always compared me to her nieces, but most importantly, we were missing the biological connection that some mothers and daughters have simply because of that blood-relation bond.

Though I am grateful that she was able to take me in and raise me, I didn't find out that she wasn't my biological mother until my teens. Maybe this is another reason why I rebelled. I never felt like I had a place with anyone, and maybe having a son with this man made me feel like I finally belonged somewhere.

I met him at a strip club. That probably should have been my first clue, but like any teenage girl, I relished having the attention of this older man. He made me feel like he cared about me, and naively I believed him. I believed that having this baby would make us a family. It never really crossed my mind that he would lie to me like the others had, that he would cheat on me and make me feel the way that I did.

All of that, though, all of those emotions and betrayals and changes did not prepare me, nor did they compare in the slightest to what would happen after January 11: *"Akila Gilyard, I hereby sentence you to a suspended sentence of 10 years, 3 years of probation, and to pay $500 in restitution."*

Chapter Three

The police came knocking at my door around midnight. I had never been in handcuffs before, but there I was being placed into the back of a police cruiser.

The charges? Assault and Battery with the Intent to Kill. I would be lying if I said I wasn't scared. I was terrified. I had no idea what to expect. I just knew the nature of this was serious, there was no denying it, there was no getting around it. Even if I had the best lawyer money could buy, there was a witness and I was still covered in his blood. I don't even think trying to get away with it ever crossed my mind.

Sitting there with the investigators was stressful.

"It's not looking good ma'am," they said. "He's flatlined twice."

All I could think about was being charged with murder. Thank God for a little bit of grace and mercy that despite how deep I had cut him, I was only close to the jugular. Any closer, and he would definitely have died.

Some people may think it's crazy to think God's grace was hanging over that situation, but for the sake of me and him, I'm sure God was there.

The investigators helped me out a lot. They let me get a phone call, so I immediately called my mom. She was in a panic. "What are they saying? What do you need to do?"

I had a $5,000 surety bond, which I had to pay $500 of to get out. But either way, it gave me time to get my affairs in order. I went and got my car, went to the house, got all of my things and moved back into my mom's house. I didn't give up my parental rights to my son, but I did make sure my mom had a power of attorney to be able to take care of anything he needed while I was gone. Boy, was I going to miss him.

I'll never forget how it felt to change from my clothes into that orange jumpsuit. I felt so degraded. It could have been a moment out of a movie. I was watching my familiar clothes be taken away, smelling the familiar scent of home as they were suddenly replaced by a cold, stale jumpsuit. That was where I found myself. I was sixteen-years-old facing years of incarceration because of a man who I thought I loved. A man that I thought I wanted and needed.

At sixteen, I wanted to be a wife so bad. I wanted this fairytale that I had made up in my mind with this man that I had found myself in a compromising position, and I felt like I couldn't get out of it. I had to go through it. I had to make the best of my situation, if only for my son.

I know you're here for all the tea, coffee, and soda too. Don't worry, you'll get all that and more. But I'm not writing just because it's therapeutic or because I want to share the darkest times of my life with others for fun; I'm sharing the darkest points of my life because they were the moments I needed, the moment that helped mold and define my life. It may sound crazy to you, but without my experience in the prison system, I wouldn't be who I am today.

The dark moments we all experience in our lives don't feel good. They can be agonizing, and sometimes it feels like they will never end, like we will never have things go our way and never be as happy as we want. But those dark moments really do help encourage growth. They encourage us to take what we have and make it better, to learn from the bad that we've done and try to change for the better.

There are two types of people in this world: the ones who make mistakes, learn from them, and try to do better, and then there are those who make mistakes and keep making them out of ignorance for change.

You get to decide which you want to be, but it may take some time to learn. I can't promise it will be easy, because it wasn't easy for me. I've made more mistakes in my life than I care to admit to, but I've also learned from those mistakes more than I ever would have had I not made them. And for that, I am grateful.

You may be wondering, Akila, how was getting sent to prison good for you? And the simple answer is this: I accomplished more in prison than I ever would have if I had stayed in the real world. How do I know? Because I know who I was when I went in better than anyone. I felt like I had it all together as a sixteen-year-old high school dropout and single mother. I didn't have the motivation back then to go back to school. And as bad as I thought I wanted it then, deep down I knew that man wasn't going to marry me. I'm confident I wouldn't have desired any more out of life than what I already had, which is sad considering how young I was at the time.

I got my GED in prison. I got a job in prison. It's not the ideal for anyone, but it was one of the best things that could have happened to me. Did it suck? Yeah, for a little while. But looking back on it, it was necessary for me. I had to take care of me in prison. At the end of the day, I was the only one who had my back. And the way I saw it was I could either waste my time sitting in that cold cell, miserable and alone, or I could use that time to my advantage.

I could finish school, I could learn skills that would make the transition out of prison much easier. I could do better and work towards being better for my son. Had I not been handcuffed that night, I probably would have turned out much different than I am now. Who knows what choices I would have made, but I know that if I had been complicit in the actions of that man against me, if I had taken him back with open arms and promises that it would never happen again, then I would have stayed complicit with everything in my life. I never would have wanted for more, never would have tried to become more, and that is something I am glad every day that I did not become.

Thinking about who I would have been had I not done what I did is something I try not to do too much of. Do I want to justify the actions that led me to jail? No. Am I grateful for the strength in spirit that I was able to give myself to keep moving forward despite the situation I found myself in? Without a doubt.

You may be going through something that's pretty dark right now. Whether you feel it's darker than the things you read about my life in this book, or not as dark, that doesn't matter. There are always going to be people who have it better than us, and there are always going to be people that have it worse than us. It helps no one to compare your shit to theirs, and at the end of the day it doesn't matter.

What matters is that what you're going through, what you've been through, is dark to you. But it does get better. I know it sounds absolutely absurd right now but enjoy the process. It won't last forever. By the end of this book, you'll see that I've been through a lot in my lifetime, and I still have plenty of living to do. I've barely reached the prime of my life. No matter where you are in this moment right now, you still have more living to do.

After I was picked up by the police and spoke with the investigators, everything happened really quickly. There wasn't an investigation. It was pretty cut and dry. There was a witness, she knew who I was and what I had done. She knew where I lived. There was no trial either. In a matter of seconds, with that box cutter in my hand and rage in my mind, I had sealed my own fate and there would be no going back, no asking for a redo. I was going to prison.

Chapter Four

I can still remember it like it was yesterday. Camille Griffin Graham Correctional Institution (CGGCI).

I was so nervous when I arrived at the facility on a bus from Orangeburg County Jail. On the bus, I was shackled with waist chains and leg irons to control my movements. I was so scared to make the wrong move, fearful that I would upset someone or cause an issue that would have further consequences for me. There were so many thoughts racing through my mind, I was sweating, my heart was pounding so loud I could hear it.

I had no idea what to expect. They make it seem like a quick process in the movies, but it's really not. Processing normally takes about a month to get through. We were checked in at a men's prison; they don't show that in the movies either. TV makes everything seem so quick and simple; boys separate from girls, strip, squat, get dressed, sit in a cell and wait to get out. Don't get me wrong, it makes for good TV, but it's not like that in real life.

I was booked into the Department of Corrections slowly. Like I said, this doesn't all happen as quick as you think. Receiving takes about thirty days. You have to get a number of tests done and have to be medically cleared before they assign you. And let's not forget you are locked in your cell for twenty-three hours a day. You get one hour of free time each day where you are allowed to shower, go do recreation, or do another activity you feel you have time for in that hour. But that's all you get.

The cells aren't what you'd expect based on the movies you've seen either. It was set up like a dorm on a college campus. We actually didn't even call them cells, they were cottages. And you didn't have "cellmates," they were just your roommates.

I did a lot of crying. I can't lie. I was scared, and I didn't know what to expect. Everything and everyone just looked so scary. I was expecting the terrible experiences I saw on shows and movies. I had so many questions going through my head. What was going to happen to my son? What was going to happen to *me?* Who were these other women I was now living with, what were they in for? Would they gang up on me? Was this going to go by quick or would it feel like forever before I could see my baby again?

I had to get used to squatting and coughing after every visit. Yes, *every* visit. It doesn't just happen when you are processed. It took a while to get used to only having the ability to wash my clothes three times a week, especially since *everybody's* clothes were washed at the same time. I had to adjust my sense of normalcy in order to survive.

Was it the best living arrangement? Absolutely not. Even once I was through receiving, it still wasn't ideal. Jail wasn't like the media portrayed, but it definitely wasn't a bungalow on the beach either. When I tell people this part of my life drastically contributed to the person I am today, they don't understand how I can have such a positive outlook on what many see as an extremely negative situation.

First and foremost, I was in the wrong. Point, blank, period. We all know we've done some things in our lives that are wrong, and we don't always want to admit to that. But I was wrong.

I made the choice to chase after him, to run him off the road, and to grab the box cutter. I made those choices, so it was on me to pay the price. Maybe this was one of the reasons why I was able to turn this situation positive. I wasn't trying to fool anyone, not even myself, that I hadn't done something horrible and I think that helped me rationalize my time in jail.

The best way I can explain how I felt is this: If you've ever broken up with someone or been broken up with and then decided that you were going to spend some time focusing on yourself, that's how I felt about the situation.

I spent *a lot* of time with myself. You kind of have to, because there's not really much else that you can do when you're stuck in your cell. I did a lot of thinking and I realized that I didn't really like who I was, nor did I like the path that girl was taking me down.

I felt like if I didn't make a change, then I was signing myself up for more mistakes, more time in prison, more of my son's life missed. And I knew that I could make one of two choices. I could let this time in prison make me even more resentful of myself, of God, of the people in my life that I felt had let me down. I could continue to put myself in situations that would force me away from my son. Or, I could make a change.

I could choose to do better for myself, for my son, and I could choose to take advantage of this time in prison to do just that.

Now, before we get to the good stuff and I tell you all the things I did to change and better myself, let me tell you about a few of the things that definitely didn't help my case. These challenges made things harder for sure, but I also think they're important to note because I overcame those too.

One thing you may be familiar with because of the movies is the fact that you can get charged with additional crimes while locked up. Yeah, it's a real thing.

A lot of people will get additional charges for violence or drug abuse, but my personal experience was a little different. It's no secret at this point that I wasn't making the best of decisions. And though I had made the decision to change, this came after a stint of rebellion and adjustment to the new system I was living in.

This first incident that I was involved in I can't take full responsibility for because it was pretty bogus. However, the first additional charge I got was a sexual misconduct charge. Yeah, that's the charge you probably attribute to pedophiles and creeps, which again is why I hold that it was bogus.

At this particular point in time, inmates weren't supposed to be in other inmate's spaces. It was really a case of wrong place, wrong time. But I'll own up to the fact that I was somewhere I wasn't supposed to be. I was in another inmate's cell, literally just sitting on the bed talking, and we got caught. For whatever reason, that was deemed as sexual misconduct, though nothing sexual had occurred. At least not then.

So, what happens when you get additional charges while you're already locked up? That time, I went to solitary for ninety days. I was required to be in a cell, alone, for twenty-three hours out of the day.

This took the idea of being alone with myself and my thoughts to a whole new level. It was almost like I was in my own prison within prison. I had nothing to do for those twenty-three hours but think. If you've ever seen people in the movies stuck in solitary where they slowly start to go crazy, it's not that far off.

Maybe not as dark and wet and dingy but being by myself for so long with no other human contact except for that one hour is the most alone I've ever felt.

It's dehumanizing in a sense because of the way you're chained up. Not only was I locked in a cell for twenty-three straight hours, but I was handcuffed anytime they took me to recreation or the showers.

At this age, it was clear that I had a problem with authority. I always had. There was just something about people telling me what to do or feeling like they had power over me that didn't sit well with me.

I flowed to the beat of my own drum which got me into a lot of trouble. If you want to go into the why of this character flaw, it probably has something to do with growing up the way that I did with people who weren't even blood relatives telling me how to dress, what to think and believe, and who I could and could not be friends with. I was always being told to act a certain way to preserve myself, but when you're a kid, you want to do the exact opposite of what adults tell you to.

I'm not sure if I ever got over my issues with authority, but I definitely learned how not to let it get me in so much trouble. Those issues with authority though, they set me up for failure during my first sentence. It made things extremely difficult since my first instinct was to rebel.

When you're locked up and treated like an animal, it's hard not to see the correctional officers and guards as the enemy. That's how they saw you. I was, however, able to make nice with a few friendly faces. There was one CO in particular that really helped me, especially during my time in solitary for that first mishap.

Sometime during that first round of solitary, I got sick. Really sick. I had to be hospitalized. I had fibrocystic cysts on my ovaries that ruptured. The pain was unbearable.

Thank God it was benign. Even then, though, it ended up being a big scare for me. My time in prison had already been filled with an overwhelming sense of anxiety and a plethora of other emotions. It was a rollercoaster, for sure. Having a potential cancer scare, without any family or friends around, was tough.

I couldn't have family by my side, no matter how bad I wanted to. I had to depend on the system to take care of me. This is where that CO came in. It took place during the holidays. The only reason I remember what time of year it happened was because my family was going to try to come and see me, but they couldn't. That CO let me call them while I was in the hospital, even though I wasn't supposed to have phone privileges since I was still technically in solitary.

When you're all alone and you are struggling with the type of emotions I was, being able to talk to my family meant the world. Being able to hear their voices definitely helped while I was recovering. It gave me this new sense of hope that I had people who cared about me and were waiting for me to get out. I wanted to get better and make it through my sentence so that I wouldn't have to go through things like this alone ever again.

Eventually, I got out of solitary and ended up back in general population. Finally, I was allowed a little more human interaction.

Chapter Five

I mentioned before that I struggled with authority. Something about walking to the beat of my own drum? Well that rhythm that I danced to unapologetically led me to be the first inmate to wear the pink jumpsuit in my jail. This was meant to single out the defiant inmates, the "rule breakers" if you will. Any of the women hit with an additional charge while incarcerated were required to wear the pink jumpsuit, and I think this probably led to us being singled out for future charges. It was easy to hit the ones who were already considered trouble makers with more charges, and in some ways, it was probably meant to keep the other inmates in line.

Shortly after the pink jumpsuit was implemented, I was hit with another sexual misconduct charge. Yeah, they really liked that one. I'm sure trying to punish the sexual capacity of inmates was the easiest way to keep them in line, though it wasn't the most effective method.

Now, this time I'll admit I was in the wrong per the rules. I wasn't in the wrong place at the wrong time like the first charge. This time, I was in the wrong place, doing the wrong things. I was caught kissing my girlfriend in the bathroom.

That's all it was at the time, but still wrong according to the prison. Back to solitary I went, along with my girlfriend. Ninety days later and I was back in general population with my sporty pink jumpsuit.

Let's back up for a second though because I know better than to think you want to know how I was able to turn my life around without all the juicy details of how it all went so wrong first, so let's talk about what you thought I was just going to skim over.

Yes, I had a girlfriend in prison. I was in prison, locked up with only women, so what else was I going to do to pass the time? Of course, relationships with other inmates are definitely frowned upon as far as the guards are concerned. I believe they thought it was just something we did in the moment, and for them it was probably an easy way to implement discipline despite the little harm that had ever been caused by an inmate's relationship.

But I had always been interested in women, and now seemed as good a time as any to explore that interest. I always wondered why it was such a big deal and who it was really bothering that I had a girlfriend, but that's another discussion for another day.

With all that being said, I was with her for about a year. The dynamic was difficult, much like relationships in the real world are, but we made it work. Being in a relationship in prison was pretty much the same as being in one outside.

The guards tried to keep us apart, in much the same way that some people in the free world try to keep people apart depending on the dynamic of the relationship. To be honest though, I'd have to say it was actually a little easier to be in a relationship in prison. There were distractions, but not as many. We were right there together so it was easy to see one another, but since we lived in different dorms, if I didn't want to be bothered or wanted my space, I was free to have that as well.

We were able to casually date and have movie nights. We were old school and wrote each other letters too. It helped us pass the time and allowed for more intimate and deep conversations than we could have in general population.

That relationship was cool, but we knew we were never meant to last. She was a lifer, meaning that she would be in prison for the rest of her life. Despite her charges and despite how short of a time it was that we were together, my relationship with her was one of the reasons I was able to cope with the entire ordeal. She provided companionship.

Because I had her, I was no longer entirely alone. I was able to rely on someone, to confide in another person who was going through the same thing I was and who actually had more experience and would be able to help me. I knew I could talk to my family, but it wasn't the same. They didn't understand what I was really dealing with or thinking or feeling.

With my girlfriend at the time, I was able to create some sense of normalcy. When you're in prison, you form a sort of family unit with the people in your dorm. You see them every day, you have to share facilities and bathrooms and rooms, so why not try to get along with them as much as possible?

We all had each other's backs because we were the only people we could trust, especially when there was such a distinct separation between us and the CO's. The CO's could go home at the end of the day. They could leave and spend time with their families. No matter how much those officers complained about their work and about their time dealing with us, we all knew that they had the option to leave and we did not. The hierarchy had been established, the food chain was in place, and we were nowhere near the top.

My first girlfriend never expected me to stay committed to her, especially when I got out. The only thing she asked of me was that I would go see her daughter whenever I got out. She had gotten pregnant by a male inmate previously.

There are co-ed prisons, which most people don't know about, and she had been in one of those before coming to the one where we met. So, she wanted me to at least stay in contact with her daughter, and I eventually did keep that up for a while. To this day, I try to keep in touch with a few women I had been locked up with. I think it's important to reach out to them, to let them know that they still have someone on their side.

Going into the prison system and then coming back out is almost like a culture shock. You go from the life you knew, the life you had been raised in and the rules you knew from societal norms, into a society of its own within the walls of prison.

You have to relearn how to survive, and then it's almost like the second you get used to your new normal, you get released and have to relearn everything all over again. Staying connected with the girls I met in prison has helped us all relearn the ways of the real world, and it reminds us that we are not alone.

The thing is, I eventually learned to make the most of my time in lockup. I learned, over time, how to deal with my emotions and with the resentment and rage and rebellion I had been struggling with for so long. I learned how to spend the time that I was alone rewiring my brain in a way that I felt would help me become the person I was trying so hard to be. I wanted to do better. I wanted to be the best that I could be for my son and for myself. I owed it to myself to do better, so I spent a lot of time thinking about that and about how I can do that.

At the end of the day, my relationship didn't work out, and we broke up before I even got out.

But that doesn't take away from how helpful and important and necessary it was for me to have that person on my side and guiding me through my time in prison. She helped me find my place within the system, and she helped me not feel so alone. She was a friend, and for that I will forever be grateful.

Beyond relationships and friendships, there weren't many real responsibilities I had in prison, not like I would have had in the real world. It gave me the opportunity to be with myself. I attribute becoming a better person to prison because so many things wouldn't have happened had I not gone.

I probably wouldn't have gotten my GED, and I know this because I know how I was when I was sixteen. I didn't want more for myself because at the time I believed that what I had was all that I was going to have. I wouldn't have wanted more for myself or my situation, nor would I have taken the time to.

Let's be honest, I was young and taking care of a baby. I wouldn't have had the time to go back to school. I probably wouldn't have had the money to pay for childcare and also take classes. Nor would I have probably wanted to.

And I can't really know for sure that my relationship with God would have progressed the way it did. I grew up in a church that placed strict rules upon its female members, but it wasn't the best way to experience God for myself.

I was forced to believe something that I didn't have a full knowledge or understanding of. My time in prison actually helped me with that though. We had volunteers who would come and do church services with us. Every now and again, we also had something called "Kairos" which translates to "of god's love."

Kairos was a whole weekend retreat when we got food from outside and were able to learn more about who God was and what that meant for each of us individually. We were never forced to believe a certain thing or look at God in a certain light, and I think that helped me realize that it was okay for me to form my own opinions about God and about my own beliefs and views on religion.

For the first time, I was allowed to think about God for myself. I was allowed to explore what that meant to me. In a way, this allowed me to reclaim some of my power back that others had tried to take away from me. I was so young when all of this was happening, so impressionable and looking for guidance, and it's ironic that I was given that freedom to explore my religion while locked up in prison.

I would never wish my experience on anyone, but at times I feel like it was absolutely critical for me to go through this so that I could develop my relationship with God. Trust me when I say the worst parts of your life can end up being the best times for your growth looking back.

Chapter Six

My first sentence felt like it lasted a lifetime, but when it was coming to an end, I started to feel this immense relief that I would soon be out.

I was so excited to be able to see my son and to start my life again. In my mind, I had already started to form ideas and plans for our future. There were things I wanted to do and see, and I was excited to be able to build a bond with my son that wasn't exactly easy to do while locked up.

Of course, though, as with life there are always obstacles standing in the way of the things that we want, and unfortunately at this time in my life I was still dealing with some impulse control problems that led me to a lengthened sentence that first time.

You remember how I told you my girlfriend and I never intended to be long term right? Like I said before, she was in for life and she never anticipated that I would keep that commitment once I got out.

We broke up closer to the end of my sentence, and I actually started talking to a different girl. Here's where things got a little interesting. You would think I would have learned how to deal with my emotions better by this point, but not so much. Learning to control the deepest and darkest parts of you takes time, and though I felt like I had done a lot of soul searching and changing, I wasn't perfect.

This particular young lady that I started talking to was actually booked and locked up with her former girlfriend. They came in together and one day, about a month or two before I was set to get out, I was in the yard when I saw the two of them frolicking around the yard together.

At this point, everyone knew that me and the girl had been talking, so seeing them together made me feel disrespected. I couldn't control my temper. The compound was closing, and I told the post officer I was about to smack her. I honestly didn't think that particular post officer was going to do anything because we were cool.

I was wrong. Either way, I walked straight up to her, my girlfriend, and I smacked the shit out of her. I just wasn't okay with that level of disrespect, or what I had deemed as disrespectful at the time.

That incident, however, and my lack of self-control cost me an additional month. The post officer called the lieutenant, something I really didn't expect her to do, and I ended up back in solitary.

The reason why I bring this incident up is to show you how difficult it was for me to control my emotions at the time. I was still so young, I was still dealing with my trust issues and with feeling betrayed by the people in my life that I had deemed important to me.

This was another incident where someone that I had connected with romantically decided to betray my trust and disrespect me, and I think because of that and because of the way that people act in jail, I felt that I needed to show treating me like that wasn't okay.

Maybe in a way it was self-sabotage since I knew I was going to be getting out soon and the idea of having to reacclimate to the real world was scary, but I think it was another instance that proved to me I still needed to work on myself and on the things I didn't like.

Chapter Seven

When I was finally out, I remember my mom coming to pick me up. It was such a bittersweet moment. I remember being so happy to see her, to be able to hug her. I got to sit in a car for the first time in a long time without having cuffs and chains attaching me to the seat. I remember what it felt like, leaving in my own clothes, feeling the sun beating down on my face, smelling my freedom in the air.

Of course, everyone loves their freedom. Every day we fight for our rights and our freedoms. It's something that we value in this country, and it is also something that we take for granted.

When you're locked up, you have to change your way of thinking because your main goal is to survive. It's horrible, but the system breaks you down until you feel like nothing more than an animal in a cage at the zoo, staring back at the ones on the outside of the cage, waiting to be free.

You become accustomed to a certain lifestyle, routine and hierarchy that dictates every move you make and every word that comes out of your mouth. You are totally at the mercy of the correctional officers and other inmates.

One wrong move and you can end up increasing your sentence, as you saw in my experience, or you can end up hurt and scared for your life. When you're released, you have to change the way you think again, and it can be extremely difficult to do. Even interacting with people on the outside is weird because social norms on the inside are so different.

It took me about a month to find a job. It might seem like common sense, but one thing they don't tell you when you get out is just how few options you have when it comes to a career, especially when you have such severe and specific charges like mine.

Not a lot of people wanted to take the chance on someone with charges of Assault and Battery with Intent to Kill. I was thankfully able to get a job at a local warehouse working the 3rd shift, and my main goal at the time was to save up so I could get my own place, because to be completely honest with you, living at home was making my transition into the real world ten times more difficult than it needed to be.

Living with my mom just wasn't cutting it. It got to the point where we were having arguments left and right because she wanted me to act and think and talk a certain way. She was a bible-thumping, fire and brimstone type of lighting, and I just couldn't get down with the idea of being in my twenties and having a 10 p.m. curfew.

Now don't get me wrong, I know I was young when I got arrested, and I hadn't made the best decisions up to this point regarding my life. But regardless, I was still grown. I had spent so much time growing up in one of the hardest places to grow up in, I had been independent for years, and the idea of having a 10 p.m. curfew as if I was still in prison did not sit well with me. It was almost like she was trying to reclaim the years of raising me that had been taken away from her, but I think what she forgot was that those years had been taken away from me too.

Because of my choices, I never got to go to prom. I never slow danced with a boy in a pretty dress and laughed with my friends about who was dating who. I never got to walk across that graduation stage. I didn't get my license like teenagers traditionally do, I didn't wake up the morning of my 16th birthday to a new car. The years that I should have spent doing reckless teenager things with my friends had been taken away when I got pregnant, when I dropped out, and ultimately when I was taken to jail. Not to mention, who knows if the church would have even allowed those things in the first place.

At the end of the day, though, I was the one who had always taken care of me. When I got pregnant and had my son, I took care of me. When I was locked up and left to fend for myself, I took care of me. I was the one who got through my sentence on my own. Sure, I had some help and guidance from time to time, but it was me who did all of that and it was me who came out of it on the other side.

I ended up moving out as soon as I could. It took me about another month to find a place to live after I moved out of my mom's house. In the meantime, I pretty much laid my head wherever I could. Really, as far as I was concerned, I had been in worse situations and this was just another obstacle in the road that needed to be dealt with.

My son ended up staying with my mom because she felt that I wouldn't be able to provide for him in the way that she could. It was hard, I'm not going to lie. Realizing that things wouldn't go back to normal immediately and that I wouldn't be able to have him with me constantly was difficult for me to deal with. But I knew that I needed to get right with myself, with God, before I would be able to provide him all the things I wanted to give.

I knew that I needed to work as hard as I could, save up to find us a nice place, and be able to continue to provide for him no matter what.

During this time, however, I met a new guy and he quickly became my boyfriend. Not much later, I found out I was pregnant. For some reason, I was okay with this. The thing about this man was that he didn't care about my past. He didn't care about what I had done. He didn't care about the fact that I had just been released from prison.

I don't think I thought about it too much at first when I got out, but I think most people are concerned with whether or not a future partner will accept them, flaws and all. It just so happened that my flaws included prison time. So, in a way, I felt like I could be myself with him because he accepted a part of me that I wasn't going to try to hide.

Typing all that though made it seem like our relationship was much more romantic than it really was. You see, I met him in a strip club. Not your typical romance movie meeting, but it's how my story goes, and I think we meet people for a reason, and if I hadn't met him then I wouldn't have my kids.

Things escalated quickly in our relationship, even though I'm not quite sure how. A lot of the events in my life happened so quickly that it's hard to pinpoint an exact moment in time or a perfect sequence detailing the events, but I won't lie.

I'm not going to downplay the things that I have done wrong in my life, and I will never claim to be a perfect woman or to always do the right things. I'm human. Humans make mistakes, and I think we forget to allow ourselves some grace because the right choices and the right paths are not always clear cut and labeled for us.

That being said, though, I take full responsibility for what I have done in my life, poor decisions and all. We did end up getting married relatively quickly. Maybe I was grasping at the first person who claimed to love me, maybe I was scared to be completely alone. Who knows the real psychology behind why we do what we do, but like I said, I'm not perfect and I did my fair share of things after I was released that made my life a little more difficult than it probably needed to be.

I did end up cheating on this man. I didn't deny it, and I never have. But we had infidelity issues that led to other issues in our relationship, and I don't really fault either one of us for them.

One specific night I was texting my cousin, but as I said I had already proven myself to be unfaithful, so he thought it was someone else. He choked me out. Hands around the throat, barely able to breathe.

Throughout our relationship, we fought a lot. At the beginning, I kind of just took everything. It's not like I wasn't used to this kind of treatment from a man, and at first, I reverted back to that fifteen-year-old girl who just wanted to be loved and would let those things happen simply because she wanted to be loved.

But then I remembered who I was, and I wasn't going to take that kind of abuse lying down. Eventually, I started fighting back. I wasn't going to be anyone's personal punching bag.

The way I saw it, if he wanted to hit me then I guess I could hit him too. But what's funny about the instance of me getting choked out is literally right after that, in the car, he said, "Do you want to get married?"

I think people try to overcompensate for their bad actions, and I think he believed that by asking me to marry him, I would look past the abuse. Looking back on it, I think I said yes in that moment out of fear more so than out of love.

Don't get me wrong here, I did believe that I loved him at that time. But I think I was more infatuated with the idea of being married than I was in being with that particular man himself. I wanted to be able to say that despite everything I had done and everything I had gone through, I had a husband. Someone loved me enough to want to marry me, and my past wasn't a factor in our relationship.

And things did work between us for a while. But this isn't where the ups and downs of my story ends. Our lives did get a little crazy and there came a point where I felt like I needed to provide more. I felt like what we had wasn't enough, and I didn't like the feeling that I was struggling.

I wanted to make something of myself and of my family, and I felt great emotional distress at where I was and what little I had to show for it. This led me to connecting with a different man. To be honest with you, the sex was just extra. The affair was more mental than it was physical. My husband didn't know any of this at the time, and eventually the man's wife became involved in our affair as well.

The problem wasn't really the affair itself. Everything else was wrong. Let me explain. I was at a point where I felt like my family didn't have enough, and this led me to a place where I felt like I was constantly in survival mode. I felt like I had to go above and beyond, by any means necessary, to ensure that my family was good.

Some might assume that taking care of the family financially is supposed to be the man's job? And to some degree I believe that it is, but the problem was that I didn't have the best track record for going about things the right way. I had been so independent for so long and I have always been the one to take care of myself that I felt this overwhelming need to ensure my family had more than enough on my own. Because of this, the affair with that couple turned into much more.

At some point, the guy showed me how to make some extra money on the side. Let's go ahead and say that it was not a legal way to make money. Now we get to the part in my story where I tell you how my affair, and the things associated with my affair, landed me in jail for the second time.

More specifically, I became involved in a credit fraud ring. Now before we go any further, let me go ahead and tell you, if your credit has been stolen, it was not me. I promise. Let me explain to you exactly how it worked.

I'm about to tell some secrets that some people probably wouldn't want me to share, but what's done in the dark always comes to the light eventually, right?

Now keep in mind, I don't really have all of the specifics. I was the low man on a very large totem pole. I can only explain what I knew specifically based on what I was doing. A lot of the other stuff was already done well before things got to me. Like I said, low man on the totem pole.

Essentially, we would get prepaid cards, the kind that were actually attached to people's bank accounts back then. We would go to the store and then buy gift cards with those prepaid cards. I honestly don't even know if you can still do that, but back then you could. So essentially, by the time the person reports fraud on their bank account, the money was already spent on a gift card and then those gift cards could be used because they were no longer tied to the original prepaid card. I honestly came in at the tail end of the operation, but I later found out that it had been going on for years.

Once I started working with these people, money was never an issue. I had whatever I wanted, my husband had whatever he wanted, and my kids were always taken care of. You couldn't tell me anything. If you were to ask me back then, I probably would have told you that my life was good. But things are always good until we get caught, right?

I did this for about a year. What I didn't know was the whole ring was being investigated long before I came along. A case had already been built. My husband didn't know about any of the specifics. He was benefiting from everything that I was doing, and it would be naïve of me to think that he was completely unaware that I was bringing in extra money.

There was no way we could be married, living in a house together, and he wouldn't have any idea that something shady was going on. Neither one of us made the kind of money we were actually spending. But he never complained about the extra cash, never complained about the things we were able to do and buy now that I was making more, so he never asked me where the money was coming from.

Needless to say, eventually my actions caught up with me and I was busted. This brings me to my second sentence. Oh, I know. You're probably thinking, but Akila, you said going to prison helped you the first time. You said it helps you be better. In a lot of ways, it most certainly did. But Rome wasn't built in a day, right?

I still made a number of choices in my life that landed me in places that I didn't have to be. I can accept that. I can also accept that regardless of what it looks like on the outside, I learned a number of lessons during both sentences. And yes, while I did go back after getting out the first time, that doesn't take away from the things I learned about myself when I was in prison. We all make mistakes, and we all make decisions. Mine just happened to have landed me in jail, twice. But going in this second time was a little different.

Chapter Eight

Like I said before, I was a small fish in a very large pond. To put that into perspective for you, I had twenty-three other co-defendants. If you don't know what that means, it basically means I was one of twenty-four people who were charged for this crime. Yeah, that's kind of a lot.

Being arrested that second time was completely different than it was the first time. I can't say that I didn't know it was coming, because I had a feeling. I might have been young, and I might have made some mistakes, but I wasn't dumb. I knew what I was doing was wrong and I knew that anytime you do something wrong, you run the risk of getting caught.

The police came to my house and confiscated everything that I had. When I was interviewed and booked, the entire process was kind of the same as before. Nothing too special there. Instead of having a public defender, I did actually pay for a lawyer this time which definitely helped me to get a lighter sentence. I had a mandatory minimum of twenty-four months. Now let's get to the things that made this time around a little more interesting.

I actually surrendered to an institution which basically means that on a specific day, I went directly to the institution where I was going to be held and turned myself in. The benefit of that for me was the fact that instead of going to prison right after my sentence, I was given one month to get my affairs in order.

From the time I was sentenced to the time I actually walked into the institution, I had a month. One final month of freedom. But let's talk about what happened on the day that I turned myself in, shall we?

On the day I was actually sentenced, I noticed that I hadn't had a cycle in a while. I was late. I went to the dollar store and got a test. I also ran into a McDonald's and got a cup. That part's kind of funny looking back on it. I took the test, and there they were, two pink lines.

I was pregnant. Again. This is what made my second time around completely different than the first.

You remember that the whole reason I'm in this mess is because I got caught up with the guy that I was having an affair with, right? In case you're not putting two and two together, this baby wasn't my husband's. He pretty much knew the baby wasn't his. I mean, we hadn't been intimate with one another in a while. Regardless, going into prison, my husband knew there was a strong possibility that the baby did not belong to him.

I honestly don't know what other women feel like when they get pregnant and aren't 100%

sure who the father is. I don't even know what I felt in those moments. I mean come on, there was kind of a lot going on right?

I didn't really have time to think about that aspect of the entire situation. I was more concerned about being with child while going back to jail. This changed everything for me. What I learned but didn't adhere to after being in prison the first time, I basically had to relearn the second time around.

Going in pregnant, and everything thereafter, changed my entire mindset about life. It changed my mindset in a way that just being in prison probably was never going to do.

I was nervous, but I was mostly frustrated. I was frustrated with myself and the situation that I had put myself in. There I was, about to turn myself in, and I was pregnant. You know when you get caught doing something and you think back and wonder why you were doing it to begin with?

Don't get me wrong, I knew why I was doing it. It was quick cash. But in that moment, I couldn't help but be frustrated with how reckless I had been. I couldn't help but be frustrated with the fact that I had gotten myself into such a situation for the second time in my life.

I wouldn't have classified myself as a career criminal, because I didn't intend to go out and continue to do things that were against the law. But obviously for the second time in my life, I had allowed my emotional state and immediate gratification to put me right back in a situation I didn't want to be in. This time was worse, though, because I was pregnant.

This time, I wasn't just putting myself in danger, but I was endangering the life of my baby, and I think that's what forced me to make such drastic changes. Of course, I knew I was responsible for my other babies and my love for them has always kept me going, but the fact that I was carrying a child in prison changed my mindset immediately. It was almost as if a switch flipped inside and I started to see things (myself, my choices, my life) in a whole different light. Ultimately, I believe this is what brought me closer to God and closer to the woman that I am today.

I surrendered. My husband dropped me off, and that was that. The good thing, if there is such a thing, about this entire situation was that I was only on the yard for one month.

Chapter Nine

I'm sure if I would have stayed on the yard, things would have been fine. People, inmates, and officers alike seemed to have taken a liking to me. I think it's because I was pregnant. Because of that as well, I was able to get into the MINT program.

The MINT program is Mothers and Infants Nursing Together. I haven't seen very many shows on TV with a program like this, unless it involved miners. But yes, I was transferred to West Virginia were l was actually able to finish my time with my daughter. It was set up almost like a group home. We had dorms, and it really wasn't that bad, except for the fact that we didn't have central air.

When it was time for me to have my daughter, my husband was allowed to be right by my side during the delivery. I thought it was great that they allowed him to come, but even more so that he showed up given the circumstances surrounding my pregnancy.

We did ultimately get a paternity test done, which was completely bogus if you ask me. My affairs new girlfriend at the time actually worked where I went to get the test done. It came back that the baby wasn't his, and her response was, "What I needed it to say, it said."

That didn't matter to me that much though. The situation was what it was. I had put myself in it and I had to deal with the consequences of my selfish decisions. The fact that my husband was able to be by my side helped, and it was completely a different experience than when I had been in the hospital during my first sentence alone, not allowed to see any of my family. I was grateful that someone familiar got to be there with me during the birth of my daughter.

During my second sentence, I did pretty much everything that I would have done out in the real world except work. We would go shopping once a month for supplies for our babies, and there were other mothers taking care of their children as well. I think the only other thing that wasn't allowed that I can think of was that our kids couldn't sleep in the same room with us.

I will say it helped me a lot being surrounded by women who were going through the same thing as me. Having a baby in prison and then having to adjust to motherhood in that kind of setting is frustrating and scary and extremely difficult. Being with women who were also taking care of their children despite their sentence was so helpful to me.

Having my daughter with me during my sentence was both great and difficult all at the same time. I absolutely loved that I was able to mother her, especially considering during my first sentence I had to leave my son with my mom. But it was a strain on my family.

My boys couldn't understand why their sister got to stay with me, but they couldn't. It was definitely a difficult situation to maneuver from that perspective. I couldn't by any means be angry at the emotions that they felt, and I completely understood any potential resentment that there was. I had put us in a bad situation, and it took a toll on them too. I think that's probably one of the biggest regrets that I have.

Looking back, I absolutely matured and learned so much by being in prison, but at the same time the cost for that was very high.

How do you explain to your kids that you can keep one of them, but the rest can only see you every so often? That was probably one of the most difficult things that I had to deal with and overcome when I was in prison the second time.

The first time, obviously, was different. I didn't have to explain why one child could be with me and another couldn't. None of them could be with me, so that made it a little easier. But knowing I had my daughter with me and she was getting time with me that my sons weren't able to have, that really put a strain on my heart. And I know it was extremely difficult for them as well.

There was a bit of resentment there for a while, and I couldn't even fault them for it. Who was I to tell them how to feel given the circumstances? I think there was also probably some resentment from my first son for putting myself back in this situation, and that was another motivating factor for the changes I knew I needed to make.

I had much more time to think this go around. I also had a lot more that I needed to deal with within myself. I was maturing, quickly. What choice did I have? I actually had to raise my daughter while serving time because of my stupid mistakes. Not even my mistakes, because it wasn't an accident, it was a choice.

I definitely grew up a lot. I didn't put myself in catty situations like I did the first time. I spent so much more time with God, and I began to love the relationship that we built.

It's kind of funny, isn't it? It's pretty cliché. I had gotten myself into such a bad situation, and I was putting my family through it too. That was the time where I learned to trust God the most. I guess for most of us, we don't turn to Him until we find ourselves at rock bottom. For that reason, I'm actually really glad I hit rock bottom.

I spent more time in prayer those two years than I ever had before. I even found myself fasting. It was all so different compared to the first time I was locked up because this time, instead of just wanting to make a change, I was actively stepping towards that change. I was making better decisions, learning to control my emotions, and I was turning to God for help if I ever felt helpless.

If I didn't know anything else, I knew that God was the only one that could help me deal with the consequences of my actions. Like I just told you, dealing with resentment from my kids was a very large pill for me to swallow. Only God could help me deal with all of the emotions that I was feeling.

I didn't even know that I could feel so many emotions at one time, but I did. Had I not spent a lot of that time in prayer, fasting, and really building my relationship with God, there's no telling where or who I would be today.

If you don't get anything else from this book, if you haven't gotten anything up until this point, I want to make sure that I stand by this claim.

I got myself into situations with consequences that I was never forced to experience. I did that. I can't blame anybody else. I could have prevented all of those lost years, all of the heartache and separation from my family, by making better choices. But, if I could do the things that I did and end up the places that I ended up and still build a strong foundational relationship with God, then I know that it's not too late for you. I promise.

At times, I thought it was too late for me. I mean, look at what I had done, look at how I had acted, look at the choices that I had made and where they landed me. By all accounts, God should have ignored my call. But He didn't. If He didn't ignore *my* call, I'm sure He's not going to ignore yours. It doesn't matter what you've done, who you've done it with, or where it has landed you. God will still build a relationship with you if you want one. He will still use you, if you allow yourself to be used.

My reliance and my faith in God is 100% what took me through my second sentence and what has ensured that I stay out of prison for the rest of my life.

His guidance led me back to my family, His love has healed the bonds with my children, and His faith in me has led me to become the woman that I am right now.

The woman who is able to tell her story, as ugly and frustrating and difficult as it is, and has given me the strength to turn it into something beautiful. The lessons that we are forced to learn are hard, and in the moment it may seem unfair.

Why me? Why did I have to go through all of the things that I went through? Why did my life have to start off that way? But those lessons, if listened to and learned from, can give us the most beautiful wisdom for continuing on in ways we never imagined possible.

It's because of Him, because of my kids, because of my own resilience and strength that I am able to stand here today and tell you from my heart that you have everything you need to take your situation and make it beautiful.

Chapter Ten

Those two years came to an end quickly. It was a completely different experience. Going about my day-to-day life with my daughter, even though there were significant restrictions, was still nice. Yes, there were times where it was extremely hard, but it was definitely a more positive and hopeful experience than the first time. And I grew so much. The Akila that I was when I came out was not the same woman who signed herself in two years prior.

I got out and was released to a halfway house. For the first time, I was separated from my daughter. Since I was breastfeeding, I still had access to see her daily, but we were no longer living in the same place.

She actually went and stayed with my aunt for a while. I was at the halfway house for about two months, and then I finally got a job. Shortly after that I got an apartment. I was able to move my two youngest kids in with me, but my mom still kept my oldest.

My husband ended up moving in with me, and we tried our hardest to work things out. We tried for a while, but so much had happened that we just couldn't seem to work through our problems. I commend the couples who are able to get through the emotional rollercoaster that comes with prison. We weren't able to make it work, and that could be for a number of reasons, but we accepted it and moved on.

If you're struggling with a relationship, know that sometimes there are just some things that you and the other person can't get past, no matter how bad you want to. And that's okay. If you feel like you're at that point, go ahead and move on. But if you think it's salvageable, work until you can distinguish whether things are getting better, worse, or staying stagnant.

Everything was going well for a while. Eventually, I was able to move into a new house. Somewhere along the way, I got involved with another female, and things were going great to start out with. The problem was, I began to start seeing those toxic patterns that always seemed to get me in trouble.

Here is where I would like to celebrate my growth for a second. When I started to see those patterns, I consciously thought about how I had reacted previously to them. Knowing where I had previously ended up because of my choices, I was able to make different decisions moving forward. I had matured enough to be able to look at myself, look at my choices, and evaluate whether I was helping myself or hurting myself by making those choices.

There was no accountability in my relationship. And the problem was, I wasn't getting any help with my household bills. Now, I knew what I had done before to ensure that my household was good. That landed me in prison with a love child. And because those thoughts started to form, I knew that it wasn't okay.

Because of that, I chose to part ways from her. It wasn't the best of breakups that I've ever had. It wasn't taken well. For a while, I still communicated with her. I still allowed her to be in my space, even though I didn't reciprocate things. I just wanted to keep the drama away.

But there was one day where I looked around and saw myself going nowhere fast. I saw so many repetitive cycles and knew I couldn't allow myself to go down that road again. I didn't have anything to lose, and yet I had everything to lose.

I couldn't make the kind of decisions I had previously made. I couldn't afford to allow myself to be locked up for a third time. My kids would never forgive me. My car had been recently repossessed and that was the straw that broke the camel's back. I made some quick and difficult decisions that changed my life for the better.

We needed a fresh start. I made the decision to move us, despite having nothing. We completely moved states. For a while, we stayed in a hotel. During this period of time, I watched God open doors in my life firsthand.

There was one day where I ran into a guy that I had met before but wasn't interested in. Somehow, though, he showed up in my life again. This was no coincidence. He was the first, and only, person to offer me anything at this point in my life. He offered us a place to stay and even helped me get a new car. Things progressed, and I found myself letting my guard down with a man in ways I never had before, not even when I was married. I never felt judged. There is no "happily ever after" with this story, because it's still being written, but I can't deny that God put him in my life at just the right time.

God may position people, or even a single person, in your life at the right moment in time. It could very well be someone you've crossed paths with before, or it could be someone completely new, but when He puts them there, it's in your best interest to let things play out. Had I remembered that I was previously uninterested in this guy and allowed that to dictate how I responded to him, I could have hindered the biggest blessing for me and my kids.

It's much more than just a man, in case you missed it. God saw fit to use a person, yes, but more importantly there was a door that opened right in the nick of time, right when we desperately needed one. I just had to get to the right place and respond to the right person.

That brings me to now. I'm still figuring life out. I'm still maturing and waking up every day consciously aware of myself, my situation, and my emotions to ensure I don't put myself, or my family, back in the places I've put us in before.

I am simply allowing God to move in my life and He has opened doors in my relationships, my career, and has even inspired me to be used to help others.

In 2021, I'll officially be launching "Unveiling Colors," a Women's Transitional Center in Atlanta that will provide programs, resources, job assistance, and a place to stay for women who have recently been released from prison.

My story could have ended like so many others, but it didn't. It doesn't even end here with the end of this book.

My book is still being written. To be quite honest, I think the second half is going to be much better than the first. Though all the juicy, drama filled details are fun to read about, I am excited to be used by God and see where it takes me. That's why I wrote this book. I want the intermission of your story to be more like mine and less like some other men and women who haven't taken a more positive turn.

You can still do it. Whatever that thing is, you can do it. It doesn't matter what you've done, if you're willing to put in the work, you can achieve anything.

I'm rooting for you. I am excited to see how your story unfolds, how it may shift and change, how a business idea may produce greatness, how your relationship succeeds.

No matter what part of your story you're in right now, it will get better. Find the lesson. It may not feel good, but there's surely one there. Don't be like me and have to take the test over again. Learn and apply it the first time.

My inmate number has turned into my largest investment to date. No, it's not a monetary number, but it has supported me. The things I learned as an inmate have taught me things that I can now share with others. The time I had to invest as a consequence of my poor choices will now benefit other women. It now benefits my relationship with God, and overall, the harvest from that investment has been difficult but rewarding.

You have a purpose. What will you do with it?

About the Author

Akila Gilyard is a woman who has seen it all. From growing up in a restrictive church to having a baby while incarcerated, she has experienced things most never will. At a young age, she was forced to take on the role of mother, protector, and she was forced to come to grips with the mistakes that took away her freedom more than once.

Despite all her struggles, Akila has taken those experiences and turned them into a book, hoping to inspire others struggling not to give up. In this book, Akila has poured her heart and soul into telling her story in hopes that her story can serve as a lesson for those needing some guidance.

She talks about what happened the day that her entire life changed, she explores the emotional roller coaster her life became, but ultimately she shows the triumph of overcoming those obstacles and creating something beautiful out of it!

akilageelifecoach.info

 facebook.com/akilagee

 twitter.com/AkilaGee

 instagram.com/coachakilagee

Notes